41 Alzheimer's Preventing Meal Recipes:

Reduce the Risk of Alzheimer's Disease the Natural Way!

By

Joe Correa CSN

COPYRIGHT

© 2016 Live Stronger Faster Inc.

All rights reserved

Reproduction or translation of any part of this work beyond that permitted by section 107 or 108 of the 1976 United States Copyright Act without the permission of the copyright owner is unlawful.

This publication is designed to provide accurate and authoritative information in regard to the subject matter covered. It is sold with the understanding that neither the author nor the publisher is engaged in rendering medical advice. If medical advice or assistance is needed, consult with a doctor. This book is considered a guide and should not be used in any way detrimental to your health. Consult with a physician before starting this nutritional plan to make sure it's right for you.

ACKNOWLEDGEMENTS

This book is dedicated to my friends and family that have had mild or serious illnesses so that you may find a solution and make the necessary changes in your life.

41 Alzheimer's Preventing Meal Recipes:

Reduce the Risk of Alzheimer's Disease the Natural Way!

By

Joe Correa CSN

CONTENTS

Copyright

Acknowledgements

About The Author

Introduction

41 Alzheimer's Preventing Meal Recipes: Reduce the Risk of Alzheimer's Disease the Natural Way!

Additional Titles from This Author

ABOUT THE AUTHOR

After years of research, I honestly believe in the positive effects that proper nutrition can have over the body and mind. My knowledge and experience has helped me live healthier throughout the years and which I have shared with family and friends. The more you know about eating and drinking healthier, the sooner you will want to change your life and eating habits.

Nutrition is a key part in the process of being healthy and living longer so get started today. The first step is the most important and the most significant.

INTRODUCTION

Alzheimer's disease is a devastating brain disease. Alzheimer's begins as simple forgetfulness. Gradually, over time the disease can destroy speech and comprehension in addition to causing restlessness and dramatic mood swings. While this is difficult for loved ones, these symptoms are more difficult for the patient. However, with the right diet the onset of Alzheimer can be delayed and lower the risk of Alzheimer's.

The diet change is simple. Increasing consumption of omega-3s, vitamins A, B, C, E, and K, and foods rich in folate, phosphorous, magnesium, and selenium. These foods include nuts, seeds, leafy greens, and fish. Many spices, such as curry and turmeric contain several of these essential vitamins allowing food to explode with flavor. Use these recipes to reduce the risk of Alzheimer's disease and as a guide for a healthier diet and life style.

41 ALZHEIMER'S PREVENTING MEAL RECIPES: REDUCE THE RISK OF ALZHEIMER'S DISEASE THE NATURAL WAY!

1. Asian Stuffed Zucchini Delight

Packed with magnesium and other essential vitamins and minerals, this stuffed zucchini helps with memory retention. The body uses magnesium in over 300 different ways, 50 of which are in the brain. Foods, such as this Asian Stuffed Zucchini, allow neural plasticity, preventing damage and improving memory.

Ingredients:

- 2 medium zucchini
- 1 pound lean ground beef
- 2 tablespoons sesame oil
- 2 cups shredded bok choy
- 1 teaspoon ginger powder
- 1 clove garlic, minced
- 1/2 teaspoon black pepper

- 1/8 teaspoon kosher or sea salt
- 2 tablespoons hoisin
- 4 green onions, diced
- 1 tablespoon chopped fresh cilantro

How to prepare:

Preheat oven to 375 degrees.

Remove stem from zucchini and slice each in half vertically. Scoop out seeds, creating a boat. Toss seeds and set aside zucchini boats.

Cook ground beef over medium-high heat, breaking up as it cooks. Cook until the beef loses its pink color and is cooked through. Drain off any fat.

In a separate pan, heat sesame oil. On medium heat, add bok choy, ginger, garlic, pepper, salt, hoisin sauce, and half of the green onion. Cook until the bok choy just beings to wilt. Add beef to mix and combine.

Evenly distribute mixture into zucchini. Bake on a parchment lined baking sheet for 10 minutes or until hot.

Remove from the oven and top with remaining diced green onion and chopped fresh cilantro.

Total calories: 320

Vitamins: Vitamin A 111µg, B-6 0.5mg, B-12 0.3µg, Vitamin C 31mg, Vitamin K 56µg,

Minerals: Calcium 121mg, Iron 2mg, Potassium 773mg, Magnesium 80mg, Niacin 4mg, Phosphorus 243mg, Riboflavin 0.3mg, Selenium 21µg, Thiamin 0.5mg, Zinc 3mg

Sugars 1.7g

2. One Pot Taco Skillet

Combining black beans and brown rice produce a complete protein. A complete protein contains all nine amino acids, which prevents brain shrinkage. This simple recipe will keep you full while ensuring a multitude of nutrition and will keep your brain healthy and strong!

Ingredients:

- 1/2 pound extra lean ground beef
- 1/2 cup cooked black beans
- 1 cup salsa, preferably homemade
- 2 cups long grain brown rice, cooked
- 1/4 cup shredded cheddar cheese
- 1 tablespoon fresh cilantro, chopped

How to prepare:

In a large nonstick skillet, cook ground beef until cooked through, breaking up the meat as you go. Drain off any access fat. Add beans and salsa, allow to simmer until beans are hot. Add cooked rice. Simmer until mix thickens slightly as the moisture from the salsa cooks off.

Remove from the heat and toss in cheddar cheese. Top with chopped cilantro, if desired.

Total calories: 263

Vitamins: Vitamin A 25µg, B-6 0.4mg, B-12 1.4µg,

Minerals: Copper 218 µg, Iron 2mg, Magnesium 71mg, Niacin 5mg, Phosphorus 245mg, Selenium 20µg, Zinc 4mg

Sugars 2g

3. Vegetable Packed Lasagna Rolls

A variety of vegetables make this lasagna entree full of vitamins and minerals to keep your brain alert and active. Each roll is the perfect serving size for an individual dinner or an addition to a family meal.

Ingredients:

- 1 (24 ounce) marinara sauce, preferably homemade
- 1 tablespoon olive oil
- 1 medium yellow onion, sliced
- 1 1/2 cups broccoli, chopped
- 1 cup mushrooms, minced
- Kosher or sea salt to taste
- 2 cloves garlic, minced
- 1 cups kale, chopped
- 1 1/2 cup ricotta cheese
- 1 1/2 cups shredded mozzarella
- 1 egg white
- 1 teaspoon fresh oregano, chopped
- 1 teaspoon fresh basil, chopped

- 1/2 teaspoon black pepper
- 12 whole wheat lasagna noodles, cooked
- 1/4 cup grated parmesan cheese

How to prepare:

Preheat oven to 425 degrees. Coat a 13" x 9" x 2" casserole dish with non-stick spray and spread 1 1/4 cups of marinara on the bottom of the dish.

In a large skillet, add oil and heat on medium-low. Sauté onion until onions are soft and begin to brown. Add broccoli, mushrooms, and pinch of salt. Mushrooms will begin to release water, cook until this water evaporates, about 2 to 3 minutes. Add garlic and kale, sauté until kale is wilted, about 3 minutes. Remove from heat and cool.

In a large mixing bowl, combine ricotta, 1 cup mozzarella, cottage cheese, egg white, oregano, basil, and pepper.

On a work surface lined with parchment paper, arrange lasagna noodles flat, add 1/4 cup cheese mix, spread evenly to cover noodles. On top of the cheese, evenly spread 1/4 cup of cooked vegetables. Start rolling the noodle at the end closest to you. Place lasagna rolls seam side down, not quite touching, in the prepared casserole dish. Evenly spread 1 cup marinara over rolls, sprinkle with remaining mozzarella and parmesan.

Cover with aluminum foil and bake 20 minutes, or until cheese is hot and bubbly. If desired, serve rolls with additional heated marinara.

Total calories: 532

Vitamins: Vitamin A 413µg, B-6 0.6mg, B-12 1.4µg, Vitamin C 76mg, Vitamin K 300µg

Minerals: Copper 850 µg, Iron 4mg, Magnesium 97mg, Niacin 9mg, Phosphorus 599mg, Selenium 46µg, Zinc 4mg

Sugars 12g

4. One Pan Chicken and Broccoli

Loaded with vitamins C and K, this easy one pan dinner helps increase energy, reduce your risk of stroke, and improve memory! Broccoli makes this a powerful anti-oxidant rich entrée anyone can enjoy.

Ingredients:

- 4 cups broccoli florets
- 4 tablespoons water
- 2 boneless and skinless free-range chicken breast
- 1 clove garlic, smashed and minced
- 1/2 teaspoon dry thyme
- 1/4 teaspoon ground rosemary
- 1/2 teaspoon ground sage
- Kosher salt
- Ground black pepper

How to prepare:

Preheat oven to 375 degrees.

Lightly spray baking sheet with non-stick spray. Place the broccoli evenly on the baking sheet and drizzle water on top of broccoli.

On top of the broccoli, place chicken breast. Sprinkle remaining ingredients on top of chicken.

Bake 15 to 20 minutes until chicken reaches an internal temperature of 165 degrees and no pink remains.

Total calories: 178

Vitamins: B-6 1mg, Vitamin C 96mg, Vitamin K 118μg

Minerals: Potassium 664mg, Niacin 9mg, Phosphorus 271mg, Selenium 31μg

Sugars 0g

5. Caprese Stuffed Portabella Mushroom

High in vitamin E, this stuffed portabella mushroom is the ultimate brain protector. The most potent of all amino acids, vitamin E allows body and brain to return to normality and protects the body and brain from stress while providing energy.

Ingredients:

- 3 tablespoons extra virgin olive oil, divided
- 1 garlic clove, minced
- 2 large portabella mushrooms, stems and insides removed
- Kosher salt
- 1/2 cup spinach
- 1 cup tomatoes, diced
- 2 ounces fresh part skim mozzarella cheese
- 2 teaspoons balsamic vinegar
- 1 tablespoon fresh basil, chopped

How to prepare:

Preheat oven to 350 degrees.

Combine two tablespoons of olive oil and garlic. Brush on inside and outside of portabella mushrooms, sprinkle with salt.

In sauté pan, heat remaining olive oil on medium heat. Sauté spinach until wilted. Spoon half the spinach into each mushroom. Top with diced tomato followed by mozzarella.

Place filled mushrooms on cookie sheet sprayed with non-stick cooking spray. Bake for 15 to 20 minutes until cheese is melted and beginning to bubble. Mushrooms should be soft. Drizzle with balsamic vinegar and sprinkle with chopped basil

Total calories: 310

Vitamins: Vitamin D 9μg, Vitamin E 4mg, Vitamin K 62μg

Minerals: Phosphorus 223mg, Selenium 21μg, Niacin 5mg

Sugars 6g

6. Turkey Burger with Avocado Relish

Avocados contain the right combination of healthy fats and vitamins to encourage and improve cognitive brain function; including memory and concentration. Supporting healthy blood flow, avocados also help improve cholesterol and can prevent strokes. Topping this juicy turkey burger with fresh avocado relish is not only creamy and delicious, but healthy brain food!

Ingredients:

- 6 ounces ground turkey
- Pinch of cayenne pepper (more if spicier is desired)
- 1/4 teaspoon smoky paprika
- Kosher salt
- 1/2 avocado
- 2 tablespoons onion, minced
- 1 tablespoon jalapeno, minced
- 2 teaspoons fresh lime juice
- 1 tablespoon fresh cilantro, chopped
- 1 whole wheat hamburger bun

- 1 slice Monterey jack cheese
- 1/4 cup fresh baby arugula

How to prepare:

Light and heat grill to medium low heat.

In small bowl, lightly mix turkey, cayenne, paprika, and salt. Form into a patty no more than 3/4 inches thick. Press thumb in center of patty so the burger will not bulge in the middle. Lightly spray each side of the burger with non-stick spray. Place on grill and grill each side approximately 6 minutes or until no pink remains in the center.

For the avocado relish, lightly mash avocado. The avocado should be creamy but slightly lumpy. Add onion, jalapeno, lime juice, and cilantro. Mix until combined.

To assemble, place burger on bun. Top with cheese, avocado relish, and arugula. Serve.

Total calories: 304

Vitamins: Vitamin B6 .4mg, Vitamin B12 1μg

Minerals: Phosphorus 280mg, Selenium 32μg, Niacin 6mg, Zinc 3mg, Riboflavin 0.3mg

Sugars 3g

7. Super Green Salmon Salad

The combination of crisp greens and flaky salmon create the perfect blend of Omega 3 and B vitamins to encourage the best brain function possible. The B vitamins keep memory sharp and nerves protected while the Omega 3s allow the brain to stay fat and happy!

Ingredients:

- 1/4 cup honey
- 1 tablespoon whole grain mustard
- 1 tablespoons Dijon mustard
- 1 tablespoons extra virgin olive oil
- 1 clove garlic, minced
- 2 (4oz) skinless salmon portions
- 1/2 cup Romaine lettuce, roughly chopped
- 1/2 cup kale, roughly chopped
- 1/2 cup spinach
- 1/2 cup baby arugula
- 1/2 large tomato, cut into wedges
- 1/2 large avocado, pitted and sliced into strips

- 2 tablespoons corn kernels
- 2 tablespoons, cut into extra thin strips
- 2 strips nitrate free turkey bacon, cooked and minced

How to prepare:

Whisk together honey, whole grand and Dijon mustard, and garlic together. Pour half into a shallow dish with the salmon portions. Marinate for two hours. Refrigerate remaining half to use as salad dressing.

Lightly spray a skillet with nonstick spray and heat over medium heat. Sauté salmon until cooked through.

In large bowl, toss together romaine, kale, spinach, and arugula with desired amount of dressing. Separate in the servings bowls. Top with tomato, avocado, corn, onion, bacon, and cooked chicken. Drizzle with additional dressing if desired

Total calories: 416

Vitamins: Vitamin A 138μg, Vitamin B6 0.6mg, Vitamin B12 2.6μg, Vitamin D 8μg, Vitamin K 87μg, Folate 107μg

Minerals: Potassium 980mg, Magnesium 76mg, Phosphorus 380mg, Selenium 56μg, Niacin 10mg

Sugars 3g

8. One Pack Shrimp Bake

While the spices add a depth of flavor to this easy One Pack Shrimp Bake, the shrimp and spinach add essential Omega 3's and Vitamins. These Omega 3's and Vitamins provide increased blood flow, providing the brain with oxygen; promoting memory and concentration. Astaxanthin found in shrimp reduces the risk of brain inflammatory disease.

Ingredients:

- 1/2 teaspoon garlic powder
- 1/2 teaspoon smoked Paprika
- 1/4 teaspoon cayenne pepper
- 1/2 teaspoon dried oregano
- 1/4 teaspoon ground thyme
- 1/4 teaspoon Kosher salt
- 2 pounds raw large wild caught shrimp, peeled and deveined
- 2 cups baby spinach leaves
- 1 medium yellow onion, cut into quarters

- 2 large tomatoes, cut into quarters
- 1 pound baby red potatoes, halved
- 2 tablespoons olive oil
- 1/2 cup water
- 2 tablespoons chopped fresh parsley leaves

How to prepare:

Preheat oven to 425 degrees

Combine garlic, paprika, cayenne pepper, oregano, thyme, and salt. Mix well and set aside.

Cut turkey sausage into pieces, each about 1 inch long.

Cut four sheets of foil, about 12-inches long. Divide sausage, shrimp, spinach, onion, tomatoes and potatoes into 4 equal portions and add to the center of each foil in a single layer.

Fold up all 4 sides of each foil packet.

Sprinkle olive oil and seasoning mix evenly over the top

and gently toss to combine. Divide water amongst the four packets, about 2 tablespoons per pack. Fold the sides of the foil over the shrimp, covering completely and sealing the packets closed.

Place foil packets on cookie sheet and bake for about 12-15 minutes. Before opening packets, cut slits into the pack to allow steam to escape. Carefully open, garnish with parsley and serve.

OPTION: Instead of baking, preheat grill and placed closed foil packets directly on rake. Grill on medium low heat for about 15 minutes.

Total calories: 229

Vitamins: Vitamin A 178µg, Vitamin B6 0.4mg, Vitamin B12 1.5µg, Vitamin C 26mg, Vitamin K 113µg

Minerals: Phosphorus 365mg, Selenium 54µg, Magnesium 32mg

Sugars 4g

9. Berry Blue Grilled Chicken Salad

Out of all berries, blueberries are most beneficial. When combined with raspberries and strawberries, such as in this fresh summer salad, the combined nutrients can slow the progression of age-related brain degeneration while improving learning, memory, and motor skills.

Ingredients:

- 1/4 cup apple cider vinegar
- 2 tablespoon honey
- 1/2 cup blueberries
- 1/4 cup olive oil
- 1/4 cup raspberries
- 1/4 cup strawberries, halved
- 1/2 cup pecans, chopped
- 1 cup romaine lettuce, chopped
- 1 cup baby spinach
- 1 cup baby arugula
- 2 cups cooked chicken breast, cubed

How to prepare:

In a blender, combine vinegar, honey, and 1/4 cup blueberries. Blend until smooth, slowly add olive oil until mix is the consistency of salad dressing – set aside.

In a large bowl, combine remaining ingredients. Drizzle with a few tablespoons of blueberry dressing, toss to lightly coat.

Separate into serving bowls, serve with additional dressing if desired.

Total calories: 518

Vitamins: Vitamin A 137µg, Vitamin B6 1.3mg, Vitamin C 26mg, Vitamin K 125µg,

Minerals: Niacin 14mg, Phosphorus 420mg, Selenium 46µg, Zinc 3mg

Sugars: 24g

10. Blackened Salmon with Ginger Bok Choy

Not only is this salmon exploding with spice, it is exploding with Omega 3s and phosphorus. Phosphorus allows healthy brain cells to thrive and remain strong while improving cognitive function.

Ingredients:

- 1 tablespoon dried thyme
- 1 teaspoon garlic powder
- 1 teaspoon onion powder
- 1 tablespoon dried oregano
- 1 tablespoon smoked paprika
- 1 teaspoon red pepper
- Kosher or sea salt to taste
- 1 (6 ounce) salmon fillets
- 2 tablespoon olive oil
- 2 green onion, chopped
- 1 tablespoon ginger root, grated
- 2 cloves garlic, grated
- 2 cups bok choy, chopped

- 1 tablespoon water
- 1/2 lime, juiced

How to prepare:

Combine spices in a small bowl. Coat each side of salmon with spice mix. Allow to rest for 5 to 10 minutes.

Meanwhile, heat 1 tablespoon olive oil in large skillet on medium heat. Once hot, place salmon skin side up. Cook until fish begins to brown and turns crisp. Carefully turn salmon over and continue to cook second side until crisp. Remove from pan and rest.

In separate medium skillet, heat remaining oil. Add green onion, ginger and garlic. Cook, stirring frequently, until mix begins to brown. Add bok choy and water, continue to cook until bok choy is wilted and water is evaporate.

Serve salmon on top of bok choy and drizzled with lime juice.

Total calories: 559

Vitamins: Vitamin B6 0.8mg, Vitamin B12µg, Vitamin D 27µg, Vitamin K 57µg

Minerals: Phosphorus 832mg, Selenium 155µg, Niacin 25mg

Sugars: 1g

11. Asian Peanut Chicken Salad

Leafy greens are loaded with Vitamin C, making this Asian inspired entrée salad extra beneficial. The highest levels of Vitamin C are found in the brain and its tissues where brain energy is most frequently used. Allow this salad to regulate the neurochemicals in your brain!

Ingredients:

- 1 lime, juiced
- 2 tablespoons hoisin sauce
- 1 teaspoon honey
- 1 teaspoon ginger root, grated
- 1 clove garlic, grated
- 1/4 cup peanut butter
- 2 tablespoons rice wine vinegar
- 1 teaspoon toasted sesame oil
- 1/4 cup chopped peanuts
- 2 cups cooked chicken breast, cubed
- 1 cup bok choy, chopped
- 1 cup kale, chopped

- 1 cup Napa cabbage, chopped
- 1/2 red bell pepper, thinly sliced
- 1/2 small red onion, thinly sliced
- 2 tablespoons fresh cilantro, chopped

How to prepare:

In blender, combine lime juice, hoisin, honey, ginger, garlic, peanut butter, vinegar, and oil until consistency of salad dressing.

Combine remaining ingredients. Add a few tablespoons of peanut dressing and toss just to coat. Separate into serving bowls, garnish with fresh cilantro.

Total calories: 441

Vitamins: Vitamin A 216µg, Vitamin B6 1.2mg, Vitamin C 82mg, Vitamin K 183µg

Minerals: Niacin 14mg, Magnesium 115mg, Phosphorus 397mg, Selenium 32µg

Sugars: 9g

12. Sweet Potato and Black Bean Burrito

Beta-carotene rich sweet potatoes combined with the perfect protein of black beans and brown rice make this burrito a powerhouse of brain nutrients. Not only will the sweet potato boost memory, but your immune system as well. The sweet potato has been used to maintain cognitive development in some of the oldest cultures in the world.

Ingredients:

- 1 sweet potato, peeled and cubed
- 1 tablespoon olive oil
- 1 tablespoon chili powder
- 1 teaspoon ground cumin
- Pinch of Kosher salt
- 4 large whole wheat flour tortillas
- 1/4 cup corn kernels
- 1/2 cup cooked black beans
- 1 cup cooked long grain brown rice
- 1 cup shredded romaine

- 1 yellow pepper, sliced
- 1/2 red onion, sliced
- 1/4 cup salsa

How to prepare:

Preheat oven to 400 degrees

Toss sweet potato in olive oil, chili powder, cumin, and salt. Place on cookie sheet and roast until potatoes are soft and beginning to brown. About 15 to 20 minutes.

Place tortillas on flat surface, divide potatoes and all other ingredients equally between each tortilla. Fold in side and roll to form burrito. Serve.

Total calories: 317

Vitamins: Vitamin A 337μg, Vitamin B6 0.3mg, Vitamin C 37mg

Minerals: Phosphorus 207mg, Magnesium 6 Mg, Thiamin 0.4mg

Sugars: 6g

13. Avocado Pasta

Not only do fresh herbs add flavor to any dish, but they're packed with nutrients! Vitamins E and K, found in fresh herbs, paired with the healthy fat of the avocado make this a well-rounded and filling pasta dish.

Ingredients:

- 2 tablespoons olive oil
- 6 spears asparagus, cut into 1 inch pieces
- 2 cloves garlic, minced
- 1/2 yellow onion, sliced
- 1 cup sweet peas, fresh or frozen (thawed)
- 1 pound cooked whole wheat penne pasta
- 2 tablespoons fresh basil, chopped
- 2 tablespoons fresh rosemary, minced
- 2 tablespoons fresh oregano, chopped
- 1 ripe avocado, cut into 1/2-inch chunks
- 1/2 cup shredded Parmesan cheese

How to prepare:

In medium skillet, heat oil on medium heat. Add asparagus, garlic, and onion. Cook until onion begins to soften and add sweet peas. Add Penne, cook until penne is hot. If the pasta beings to stick to the pan, add a tablespoon of water.

Toss in basil, oregano, avocado, and parmesan. Once parmesan just begins to melt, spoon until serving bowls.

Total calories: 589

Vitamins: Vitamin B6 0.5mg, Vitamin E 3mg, Vitamin K 50μg

Minerals: Magnesium 132mg, Phosphorus 433mg, Selenium 85μg, Zinc 4mg

Sugars: 6g

14. Eggplant Lasagna

Filled with Vitamin K, this pasta-free lasagna is a brain booster. Vitamin K regulates the calcium in the brain improving overall brain health.

Ingredients:

- 1 (24 ounce) jar marinara sauce, preferably homemade
- 1 tablespoon olive oil
- 1 medium yellow onion, sliced
- 1 cup mushrooms, minced
- Kosher or sea salt to taste
- 2 cloves garlic, minced
- 3 cups spinach, chopped
- 1 cup ricotta cheese
- 1 1/2 cups shredded mozzarella
- 1/2 cup cottage cheese (small curd if possible)
- 2 egg white
- 1 teaspoon fresh oregano, chopped
- 1 teaspoon fresh basil, chopped

- 1/2 teaspoon black pepper
- 2 large eggplant, sliced 1/4 inch thick lengthwise
- 1/4 cup grated parmesan cheese

How to prepare:

Preheat oven to 425 degrees. Coat a 13" x 9" x 2" casserole dish with non-stick spray and spread 1 1/4 cups of marinara on the bottom of the dish.

In a large skillet, add oil and heat on medium-low. Sauté onion until onions are soft and begin to brown. Add mushrooms, and pinch of salt. Mushrooms will begin to release water, cook until this water evaporates, about 2 to 3 minutes. Add garlic and spinach, sauté until spinach is wilted, about 3 minutes. Remove from heat and cool.

In a large mixing bowl, combine ricotta, 1 cup mozzarella, cottage cheese, egg white, oregano, basil, and pepper.

Arrange sliced eggplant flat in casserole dish add 1/4 cup cheese mix, spread evenly to cover noodles. On top of the cheese, evenly spread 1/4 cup of cooked vegetables.

Repeat process until no cheese or vegetable filling is left, ending with eggplant on top. Evenly spread 1 cup marinara over rolls, sprinkle with remaining mozzarella and parmesan.

Cover with aluminum foil and bake 20 minutes, or until cheese is hot and bubbly. If desired, serve with additional heated marinara.

Total calories: 315

Vitamins: Vitamin A 210 µg, Vitamin B6 0.5mg, Vitamin B12 0.9 µg, Vitamin K 98µg

Minerals: Calcium 444mg, Potassium 1050mg, Riboflavin 0.5mg, Niacin 6mg

Sugars: 15g

15. Ahi Tuna Burger with Arugula and Tarragon Yogurt Aioli

A great alternative to salmon, Ahi tuna is packed with B Vitamins. The nutrients found in this fish allow for optimal oxygen circulation, providing the brain with all the resources it needs for ultimate brain function.

Ingredients:

- 1/2 pound ahi tuna, minced
- 2 tablespoons onion, minced
- 1 egg
- 3 cloves garlic, minced and divided
- 2 tablespoons ground pistachios
- 1/4 teaspoon cayenne pepper
- 2 tablespoons lime juice, divided
- 1 tablespoon sesame oil
- 1/2 cup plain Greek yogurt
- 2 tablespoons fresh tarragon, chopped
- 1/4 cup shredded cucumber
- 1/2 cup baby arugula

- 2 whole wheat hamburger buns

How to prepare:

Combine tuna, onion, egg, one clove garlic, cayenne pepper, pistachios, and 1 tablespoon lime juice. Form into patties. Patties will be very fragile.

Heat sesame oil in skillet on medium heat. Once hot, place tuna patties in pan and cook until medium and some pink remains (fish can be cooked well-done if desired).

While cooking, combine remaining lime juice, remaining garlic, Greek yogurt, tarragon. Squeeze excess water from cucumber and add to yogurt mixture.

Spread yogurt sauce on to bun, followed by tuna burger. Top with arugula and top bun. Serve.

Total calories: 416

Vitamins: Vitamin B6 1.4mg, Vitamin B12 2.8µg

Minerals: Phosphorus 559mg, Niacin 23mg

Sugars: 7g

16. Pecan Crusted Salmon with Roasted Brussels Sprouts

The trio of pecans, salmon, and Brussel sprouts make this meal a nutrient rich cornucopia. This dish is well rounded with Vitamins B, C, D, and K and loaded with Omega 3s and Niacin. Niacin slows the rate of cognitive loss, allowing improved memory and antioxidant functions of the brain.

Ingredients:

- 1 pound Brussels sprouts, stems removed cut in half
- 2 tablespoons olive oil, divided
- 1 teaspoon salt, divided
- 1/2 teaspoon black pepper
- 1 clove garlic, minced
- 2 (6 ounces) salmon filets
- 1/2 cup pecans, ground
- 1 teaspoon cayenne pepper

How to prepare:

Preheat oven to 400 degrees. Spray cookie sheet with nonstick spray.

Toss Brussels sprouts with half the olive oil, half the salt, pepper, and garlic. Place on cookie sheet and bake for 15 minutes.

Brush the salmon with remaining olive oil. Combine the pecans, remaining salt, and cayenne. Press the pecan mixture onto the salmon.

Remove Brussels sprouts from oven and turn. Place crusted salmon on pan with Brussels sprouts and return to the oven for an additional 10 to 15 minutes until salmon is flaky and Brussels sprouts are crispy.

Total calories: 757

Vitamins: Vitamin B6 0.9mg, Vitamin B12 7.8μg, Vitamin C 82mg, Vitamin D 27μg, Vitamin K 168μg

Minerals: Phosphorus 939mg, Selenium 157µg, Niacin 25mg

Sugars: 3g

17. Slow Cooker Sweet Potato Chili

Quick and easy brain food for a busy day. Sweet potato makes this meatless chili flavorful and filling. Packed with Vitamin A and C it's the perfect balance of delicious and nutritious.

Ingredients:

- 1 large sweet potato, peeled and diced
- 1 large onion, diced
- 1 jalapeno, seeds removed, diced
- 1 teaspoon garlic powder
- 3 tablespoons chili powder
- 1 tablespoon ground cumin
- 1 teaspoon smoked paprika
- 1 1/2 cups water
- 2 cups black beans
- 2 (14-ounce) can diced tomatoes

How to prepare:

Combine all ingredients in slow cooker. Cook on low for 8 hours. Serve.

Total calories: 228

Vitamins: Vitamin A 497µg, Vitamin B6 0.6mg, Vitamin C 51mg

Minerals: Phosphorus 231mg, Magnesium 96mg, Thiamin 1.5mg

Sugars: 10g

18. Slow Cooker Coconut Cashew Chicken with Vegetables

Enjoy this Asian flare with a side of essential vitamins and minerals. A large amount of B6 slows shrinkage of the brain and reduces gray matter atrophy in areas most susceptible to memory loss.

Ingredients:

- 3 skinless boneless chicken breasts
- 1 onion, diced
- 1 (14oz) can unsweetened coconut milk
- 1 cup water
- 1/2 cup ground cashews
- 2 tablespoons tomato paste
- 2 clove garlic, minced
- 2 teaspoons hoisin sauce
- 1 teaspoon turmeric
- 1/2 teaspoon curry powder
- 1/2 teaspoon cayenne pepper
- 1 carrot, peeled and diced

- 3 stalks celery, diced
- 4 red potatoes, skin on, cut into quarters
- 2 cups kale, chopped

How to prepare:

Combine all ingredients in slow cooker with the exception of kale. Cook on low for 8 hours or high for 4 hours.

Add kale, allow kale to wilt, about 5 minutes. Serve.

Total calories: 570

Vitamins: Vitamin A 314μg, Vitamin B6 1.0mg, Vitamin C 58mg Vitamin K 253μg

Minerals: Magnesium 153mg, Phosphorus 465mg, Selenium 33μg

Sugars: 10g

19. Salmon Salad Sandwich

A light meal option, this salmon salad sandwich contains selenium. Acting as an antioxidant, selenium repairs nerve cells preventing cognitive decline.

Ingredients:

- 8 ounces salmon, cooked and flaked
- 3 tablespoons plain Greek yogurt
- 2 teaspoons lime juice
- 2 teaspoon fresh tarragon, chopped
- 1 teaspoon dry dill
- 4 slices tomato
- 4 slices red onion
- 1/2 cup baby spinach
- 4 slices whole wheat bread, toasted

How to prepare:

Combine salmon, yogurt, lime, tarragon, and dill. Mix well, taste and add more seasoning if desired.

Divide salmon spread between two slices of wheat bread. Top with tomato, onion, and spinach. Place second slice of bread on top and serve.

Total calories: 345

Vitamins: Vitamin B6 0.5mg, Vitamin B12 3.3μg, Vitamin D 11μg, Vitamin K 55μg

Minerals: Phosphorus 493mg, Selenium 78μg, Niacin 13mg

Sugars: 6g

20. Greek Chicken Spinach Salad with Yogurt Dressing

Combine with spinach, walnuts make this a superfood packed salad with Mediterranean flare. Antioxidants protect against degeneration while B vitamins give brain cells energy and new life.

Ingredients:

- 4 clove garlic, minced, divided
- 2 teaspoons dry oregano
- 2 tablespoons lemon juice, divided
- 1 tablespoon olive oil
- 2 skinless boneless chicken breast
- 1/2 cup shredded cucumber
- 1 cup Greek yogurt
- 2 teaspoons dry dill
- 4 cups spinach
- 1/4 cup walnuts
- 1/4 cup feta cheese

How to prepare:

Combine 2 cloves of the garlic, oregano, 1 tablespoon lemon juice and olive oil. Pour over chicken breast. Set aside and marinate for 30 minutes. After marinating, cook in skillet on medium heat until internal temperature reaches 165 and no pink remains. Set aside to rest.

In small bowl, combine cucumber (squeezed of excess water), yogurt, dill, remaining garlic, and remaining lemon juice. Mix well.

In two bowls, divide spinach equally. Add 1 tablespoon yogurt dressing into each bowl and toss just until leaves are coated. Top with walnuts, feta cheese and chicken – serve.

Total calories: 452

Vitamins: Vitamin A 319μg, Vitamin B6 1.2mg, Vitamin K 317μg

Minerals: Phosphorus 481mg, Selenium 36µg, Riboflavin 0.5mg, Niacin 10mg

Sugars: 7g

21. Seared Salmon with Spinach and Sundried Tomatoes

This may be the simplest of recipes, packed with flavor and an abundance of vitamins and minerals. With over daily recommendations of Vitamin B12, Vitamin D, and Niacin, this easy recipe will boost your brains cognitive abilities!

Ingredients:

- 2 (8oz) salmon filets
- Salt and pepper to taste
- 1 tablespoon olive oil, divided
- 1 clove garlic, minced
- 1/2 cup sundried tomatoes, chopped
- 2 cups spinach

How to prepare:

Lightly season both sides of salmon with salt and pepper. Heat half the olive oil in skillet on medium heat. Once hot, place salmon skin side down. Cook approximately 6 minutes and flip. Continue to cook until just flaky.

Meanwhile, in a separate skillet, heat remaining oil. Once hot, add garlic and sun dried tomatoes. Cook until fragrant, about 1 to 2 minutes. Add spinach, cook until wilted. Serve on top of salmon.

Total calories: 597

Vitamins: Vitamin B6 0.9mg, Vitamin B12 9.6µg, Vitamin D 33µg, Vitamin K 84µg

Minerals: Potassium 1944mg, Phosphorus 1037mg, Selenium 191µg, Niacin 31mg

Sugars: 5g

22. Berry and Apple Salad with Cider Dressing

This crisp refreshing salad is the perfect light meal of a fall evening. A variety of leafy greens pack this salad with Vitamin K, strengthening brain cells and nerves.

Ingredients:

- 1 tablespoon honey
- 1/4 cup apple juice
- 3 tablespoons apple cider vinegar
- 2 tablespoons olive oil
- 1 cup romaine
- 1/2 cup baby arugula
- 1/2 cup spinach
- 1/2 cup kale
- 1 medium gala apple, sliced thin
- 1/4 cup blackberries
- 1/4 cup blueberries

How to prepare:

Combine honey, juice, vinegar, and oil in blender. Blend until well combine and the consistency of salad dressing.

In large bowl, combine remaining ingredients with 2 to 3 tablespoons of dressing. Lightly toss. Divide into serving bowls. Serve with additional dressing. If desired, chicken or salmon can be added.

Total calories: 234

Vitamins: Vitamin C 27mg, Vitamin K 149μg

Minerals: Folate 49μg, Magnesium 26g

Sugars: 22g

23. Chicken and Apple Spinach Wrap

Celery added to this wrap, or any dish, is a low calorie option with great brain benefit. While not changing the flavor of any recipe, celery boosts oxygen flow to the brain promoting healthy cells and overall brain function.

Ingredients:

- 1 boneless skinless chicken breast, shredded
- 1 medium apple, cubed
- 2 celery stalk, minced
- 2 tablespoons onion, minced
- 3 tablespoons plain Greek yogurt
- 2 teaspoons honey
- 1/2 cup spinach
- 2 large whole wheat tortillas

How to prepare:

Combine all ingredients except spinach and tortilla.

Lay tortillas on flat surface. Divide spinach between both tortillas, top with chicken mixture. Fold in side of tortilla and roll to form burrito shape. Serve.

Total calories: 256

Vitamins: Vitamin B6 0.6mg, Vitamin K 44µg

Minerals: Phosphorus 260mg, Selenium 28µg, Niacin 6mg

Sugars: 15g

24. Blackened Ahi Tuna with Mango Salsa and Avocado

Take a break from salmon and kick Vitamin B into high gear with Ahi Tuna! A great alternative to salmon, Ahi tuna contains enough Vitamin B to give you extra energy and improve concentration.

Ingredients:

- 1 teaspoon cayenne pepper
- 1/2 teaspoon garlic powder
- 1/2 teaspoon onion powder
- 1/4 teaspoon Kosher salt
- 1/2 teaspoon black pepper
- 1 teaspoon paprika
- 1 teaspoon chili powder
- 1 tablespoon olive oil
- 2 (6oz) Ahi Tuna Filets
- 1 large tomato, diced
- 1 small red onion, diced
- 1/4 cup mango, diced
- 1 tablespoon lime juice

- 2 teaspoon fresh cilantro, chopped
- 1 tablespoon jalapeno pepper, minced

How to prepare:

Combine cayenne, garlic powder, onion powder, salt, pepper, paprika, and chili powder. Brush tuna filets with olive oil and season well with spice mix.

Heat skillet on medium heat, place tuna in pan and cook until the first side begins to brown. Flip, and continue cooking on second side, about 3 minutes. Tuna should still be pink on the inside.

In medium bowl, combine remaining ingredients. Allow to rest for about 5 minutes. Spoon on top of cooked tuna. Serve.

Total calories: 370

Vitamins: Vitamin B6 2.4mg, Vitamin B12 4.7μg

Minerals: Phosphorus 682mg, Selenium 207μg, Niacin 43mg

Sugars: 7g

25. Peanut Chicken Lettuce Wraps

An entrée or an appetizer, this carb free favorite is loaded with Vitamin K. A key anti-aging component, Vitamin K keeps the mind sharp. By proving and regulating calcium to brain cells, Vitamin K keeps the brain functioning.

Ingredients:

- 1 pound ground chicken
- 1 tablespoon sesame oil
- 2 cloves garlic, minced
- 1 yellow onion, diced
- 2 tablespoons creamy peanut butter
- 1 tablespoon honey
- 2 tablespoons rice vinegar
- 2 tablespoons hoisin
- 1 head bib lettuce
- 1/2 cup shredded carrots
- 1/2 cup cucumber, diced small
- 1/2 cup red bell pepper, diced small
- 1/4 cup sliced green onions

- 3 tablespoons fresh cilantro, chopped

How to prepare:

In skillet, cook ground chicken until no pink remains. Drain off any excess liquid. Set aside.

In small sauce pan, heat sesame oil. Add garlic and onion. Cook until garlic is fragrant and onion is soft. Add peanut butter, honey, vinegar, and hoisin sauce. Whisk until smooth. Bring to a boil, reduce heat and simmer for 2 minutes. Gradually add to cooked ground chicken, just until all chicken is coated.

Carefully remove and separate leaves from head of bib lettuce. On each leave, spoon about 2 tablespoons chicken and top with carrot, cucumber, pepper, onion, and cilantro. Serve.

Total calories: 299

Vitamins: Vitamin A 237μg, Vitamin B6, 0.6mg, Vitamin C 31mg, Vitamin K 63μg

Minerals: Riboflavin 0.3mg, Niacin 7mg

Sugars: 11g

26. Seared Steak with Baked Tomatoes and Spinach

Strictly found in meat, this succulent steak recipe contains carnosine, which is a little known but powerful nutrient. Carnosine is created from two amino acid is found in muscles and brain tissues. Maintaining carnosine is important in preventing degenerative processes in the brain and prevents premature aging.

Ingredients:

- 2 large tomatoes
- 2 tablespoons olive oil, divided
- 2 clove garlic, minced and divided
- 1/2 teaspoon ground turmeric
- 1/2 teaspoon ground cumin
- 1/2 teaspoon chili powder
- 1 teaspoon paprika
- 1/4 teaspoon black pepper
- 2 (6oz) Sirloin steaks
- 1/2 teaspoon salt
- 3 cups spinach

How to prepare:

Preheat oven to 400 degrees. Coat tomatoes with 1 tablespoon of olive oil and half the garlic. Bake for 15-20 minutes, or until soft

Combine turmeric, cumin, chili powder, paprika, and black pepper. Coat steaks on each side with spice mix

In medium skillet, heat 1 tablespoon olive oil. On medium heat, cook steaks until medium. A little pink in the middle or internal temperature of 150 degrees.

Remove steak from pan to rest. In the same skillet the steaks were cooked in, add spinach and remaining garlic. Cook on medium heat until wilted. Serve with steak and baked tomato.

Total calories: 346

Vitamins: Vitamin A 195μg, Vitamin B6 0.9mg, B12 1.6μg, Vitamin K 161μg

Minerals: Phosphorus 317mg, Selenium 43μg, Zinc 7mg

Sugars: 2g

27. Salmon Cakes with Bok Choy and Wasabi Lime Aioli

Typically over looked, Wasabi is a great way to and a punch and nutrients to a recipe! Wasabi contains many vitamins and minerals and is known to help with inflammation.

Ingredients:

- 2 (6oz) salmon filets, minced
- 3 egg whites
- 2 teaspoons dry dill
- 2 green onion, diced
- 1 tablespoon lemon juice
- 3 tablespoons whole wheat Panko bread crumbs
- 1/2 teaspoon Kosher salt
- 2 tablespoons olive oil, divided
- 1 tablespoon grated ginger
- 2 clove garlic, grated and divided
- 3 cups bok choy
- 3 tablespoons mayonnaise
- 3 tablespoons lime juice

- 1 teaspoon wasabi paste (more if desired)
- Water, as needed

How to prepare:

Combine salmon, egg, dill green onion, lemon juice, Panko and salt. Mix well and form into patties.

In medium skillet, heat half the olive oil. On medium heat, cook the salmon patties until brown. Flip and continue to cook until done throughout.

Meanwhile, heat the remaining olive oil. On medium heat, add half the garlic and ginger. Cook until garlic just begins to brown. Add bok choy and cook until wilted.

In a small bowl combine mayonnaise, lime juice, wasabi past, and remaining garlic. Mix well. If needed, add water to make aioli the consistency of salad dressing.

Serve salmon cakes on top of bok choy. Drizzle with wasabi lime aioli.

Total calories: 626

Vitamins: Vitamin A 346µg, Vitamin B6 1.3mg, Vitamin B12 8.3µg, Vitamin C 70mg, Vitamin D 19µg, Vitamin K 122µg

Minerals: Phosphorus 557µg, Selenium 67µg, Niacin 16mg

Sugars: 5g

28. Slow Cooker White Bean Chicken Soup

A great alternative to the black or kidney beans, cannellini beans are just as beneficial. Adding a more buttery flavor and texture, this bean is very versatile in great in light soups, chilies and stews. This little bean improves cognitive ability and detoxifies.

Ingredients:

- 1 teaspoon fresh sage, chopped
- 1 teaspoon fresh rosemary, chopped
- 1 pound skinless boneless chicken breasts, cut into 1-inch pieces
- 1 small onion, diced
- 2 medium carrots, peeled and diced
- 2 large celery stalks, diced
- 2 large tomatoes, diced
- 3 tablespoons tomato paste
- 3 cups chicken bone broth
- 1 cup water
- 2 cups cannellini beans

- 2 cups kale, chopped

How to prepare:

Combine all ingredients, with the exception of kale, in slow cooker. Cook on high for 4 hours or low for 8 hours. Before serving, stir in kale and cook just until wilted. Ladle into serving bowls.

Total calories: 313

Vitamins: Vitamin A 210μg, Vitamin B6 0.8mg, Vitamin C 65mg, Vitamin K 254μg

Minerals: Phosphorus 373mg, Selenium 25μg, Niacin 13mg

Sugars: 4g

29. Shrimp Stuffed Avocado

Shrimp and avocado are a great pair, not only in recipes but in creating a meal well balanced in important vitamins and minerals. Both contain healthy fats and cholesterol to improve brain function, blood flow, and healthy brain cells and nerves. All of which work together to prevent cognitive degeneration.

Ingredients:

- 2 avocados
- 2 cups cooked shrimp, diced
- 1 celery stalk, minced
- 2 tablespoons onion, minced
- 2 teaspoon dry dill
- 1/4 cup plain Greek yogurt
- 1 tablespoon mayonnaise
- 1 teaspoon lemon juice

How to prepare:

Cut avocados in half, remove pit and scoop out a bit of the center to create a boat. Place scooped out avocado in medium mixing bowl. Skin can be left on, or removed if desired.

Mash the scooped out avocado. Combine remaining ingredients with mashed avocado. Spoon into avocado boats. Serve.

Total calories: 423

Vitamins: Vitamin B6 0.7mg, Vitamin B12 1.4µg, Vitamin K 57µg

Minerals: Phosphorus 428mg, Selenium 56µg

Sugars: 3g

30. Warm Chickpea Salad

While typically used for hummus, the chickpea is a very versatile bean. In this warm salad, the chickpea adds a post of protein while boosting memory. This salad is a great meal for improving the quality of sleep, which the brain needs to regenerate each day.

Ingredients:

- 1 tablespoon olive oil
- 1 small red onion, diced
- 1 small red bell pepper, diced
- 2 clove garlic, minced
- 1 medium tomato, diced
- 2 cups chickpeas
- 2 cups Spinach
- 2 tablespoon fresh basil, chopped
- 1/2 cup shredded parmesan cheese
- 1 tablespoon lemon juice

How to prepare:

Heat olive oil in skillet over medium heat. Once hot, add onion, bell pepper, and garlic. Cook until onions are soft. Add tomato, spinach and chickpeas. Cook until spinach is wilted and chickpeas are hot. Stir in basil and parmesan until cheese is melted. Spoon into serving plates and drizzle lemon juice on top and serve.

Total calories: 316

Vitamins: Vitamin K 115µg

Minerals: Phosphorus 293mg, Folate 159µg

Sugars: 8g

31. Taco Stuffed Bell Pepper

A great low carb alternative to a traditional taco! The blend of black beans and brown rice not only combine to make a perfect protein, but make this little pepper a filling meal.

Ingredients:

- 2 large red bell peppers
- 1 tablespoon olive oil, divided
- 1 clove garlic, minced
- 1 small onion, chopped
- 1 cup black beans, cooked
- 1 cup cooked brown rice
- 2 cups salsa, preferably homemade
- 1/4 cup fresh cilantro, chopped
- 1/4 cup shredded cheddar cheese

How to prepare:

Preheat oven to 375 degrees.

Cut off the tops of the peppers, carefully scoop out the seeds and white ribs creating a bowl. Place on cookie sheet sprayed with nonstick spray.

Heat olive oil in large sauté pan over medium heat and add onions and garlic. Mix in beans, rice, and salsa. Cook until warmed though.

Spoon mixture into peppers and top with cheese. Bake 20 to 25 minutes, until peppers are soft and filling is hot.

Total calories: 536

Vitamins: Vitamin A 325µg, Vitamin B6 1.1mg, Vitamin C 261mg, Vitamin E 8mg, Vitamin K 44µg

Minerals: Magnesium 138mg, Phosphorus 387mg, Folate 180µg, Thiamin 0.5mg

Sugars: 15g

32. Spiced Meatballs with Tomato Brown Rice

Everyone loves a good meatball. Venture out from the norm with this spiced meatball. Containing turmeric, a little known spice, makes this meatball a powerful anti-inflammatory agent. In addition, turmeric is a strong antioxidant and has shown to improve the regeneration of cells in the brain stem.

Ingredients:

- 1 cup whole wheat Panko bread crumbs
- 1 pound extra lean ground beef
- 2 egg whites
- 1 small onion, diced and divided
- 4 cloves garlic, minced and divided
- 1 teaspoon turmeric
- 2 teaspoons paprika
- ¼ teaspoon cayenne
- ½ teaspoon ground cumin
- 2 tablespoons fresh parsley, chopped
- 2 tablespoons fresh cilantro, chopped

- 1 tablespoon olive oil
- 2 cups brown rice, cooked
- 1 (14 ounce) can diced tomatoes

How to prepare:

Preheat oven to 400. Spray cookie sheet with nonstick spray. In large bowl, combine panko, ground beef, egg whites, half the onion, half the garlic, turmeric, paprika, cayenne, cumin, parsley and cilantro. Mix well and roll into one inch balls. Place on cookie sheet and bake 15 to 20 minutes.

In skillet, heat olive oil on medium heat. Add remaining onion and garlic and cook until onions are soft. Add rice and tomatoes. Cook until hot. Serve meatballs on top of rice.

Total calories: 551

Vitamins: Vitamin A 81µg, Vitamin B6 0.9mg, Vitamin B12 3.3µg, Vitamin C 24mg, Vitamin K 56µg

Minerals: Phosphorus 442mg, Selenium 49μg, Zinc 8mg, Riboflavin 1.6mg, Niacin 12mg

Sugars: 8g

33. Herb Shrimp with Couscous

Shrimp is typically thought of as a source of healthy fat and cholesterol. However, shrimp is one of the most well rounded foods. In addition, shrimp is high is antioxidants and minerals. This allows a small amount of shrimp to go a long way in brain and body health.

Ingredients:

- 2 tablespoons olive oil
- 1 red bell pepper, diced
- 1/2 pound asparagus, cut into 1 inch pieces
- 1 small onion, diced and divided
- 4 clove garlic, minced and divided
- 1 pound raw shrimp, peeled and deveined
- 2 tablespoons lemon juice
- 1 tablespoon fresh basil, chopped
- 2 teaspoons fresh oregano, chopped
- 2 teaspoons fresh rosemary, chopped
- 2 cups couscous, cooked

How to prepare:

Over medium heat, heat half the olive oil in skillet. Add red pepper, asparagus, half the onion, and half the garlic. Cook until veggies begin to soften. Add shrimp and cook until shrimp is pink and firm. Stir in lemon juice, basil, oregano, and rosemary.

In separate skillet, heat remaining oil. Add remaining onion and garlic. Cook until soft. Add couscous, mix well. Heat until hot. Serve shrimp over couscous.

Total calories: 749

Vitamins: Vitamin B6 1.8mg, Vitamin B12 2.2μg, Vitamin C 89mg, Vitamin E 9mg, Vitamin K 71μg

Minerals: Magnesium 97mg, phosphorus 535mg, Selenium 141μg Zinc 4mg

Sugars: 6g

34. Roasted Beet Salad with Orange and Walnuts

Sweet honey and orange citrus make this beet salad a wonderful earthy salad. Beets contain a high level of nitrates, which widen blood vessels and allow an increased blood flow to the brain. A healthy blood flow allows deeper concentration and higher memory capabilities.

Ingredients:

- 2 red beets, peeled and diced large
- 2 golden beets, peeled and diced large
- 2 tablespoons olive oil
- 1 tablespoon fresh rosemary, chopped
- 1 tablespoon orange zest
- 3 cups spinach
- 1 large orange, peeled and cut into wedges
- 1/4 cup walnuts
- 1/4 cup crumbled soft goat cheese
- 2 tablespoons honey
- 2 tablespoons balsamic vinegar

How to prepare:

Preheat oven to 450 degrees.

Toss both beets in olive oil, rosemary, and orange zest. Bake for 20 to 25 minutes, stirring every 10 minutes. Bake until soft. Remove from oven and cool completely.

In large bowl, toss cooked beets, spinach, oranges, walnuts and cheese. Divide into serving bowls. Drizzle with honey and vinegar to serve.

Total calories: 473

Vitamins: Vitamin A 292µg, Vitamin C 56mg, Vitamin K 238µg

Minerals: Magnesium 114mg, Phosphorus 232mg

Sugars: 38g

35. Balsamic Veggie Wrap

Balsamic vinegar gives this veggies wrap a little zip to create a wonderful light and quick meal. Packed with several different vegetables, this wrap contains a variety of vitamin and minerals to help with everyday brain function. Keeping the brain alert and energized.

Ingredients:

- 1 tablespoon olive oil
- 1 small zucchini, cut into thin strips
- 1 red bell pepper, cut into thin strips
- 1 small onion, cut into thin strips
- 1/4 cup mushrooms, chopped
- 1/2 cup spinach
- 2 clove garlic, minced
- 2 tablespoon honey
- 1/4 cup balsamic vinegar
- 2 large whole wheat tortillas

How to prepare:

In medium skillet, heat olive oil on medium heat. Once hot, combine all ingredients with exception of honey, vinegar, and tortillas. Cook until veggies are soft.

In small sauce pan, combine honey and vinegar. Cook on medium heat, bring to a boil and simmer until slightly thickened. Stir frequently.

On flat surface, lay tortillas. Divide cooked veggies between the tortillas and drizzle vinegar and honey sauce over the top. Fold in the sides and roll into a burrito shape. Serve.

Total calories: 522

Vitamins: Vitamin A 284μg, Vitamin B6 0.6mg, Vitamin C 99mg, Vitamin K 190μg

Minerals: Potassium 1047mg, Phosphorus 283mg

Sugars: 44g

36. Mediterranean Shrimp with Pasta

A spin on the popular Mediterranean diet, this shrimp pasta dish is a fresh dish overflowing with flavor. Popular Mediterranean spices, such as garlic and capers, provide extra nutrients to improve cognitive function and decrease the decline of brain activity.

Ingredients:

- 1 tablespoon olive oil
- 1/2 pound raw shrimp, peeled and deveined
- 2 clove garlic, minced
- 1 small onion, diced
- 1/4 cup zucchini, diced
- 1/4 cup eggplant, diced
- 1/4 cup capers, drained and dried
- 1 cup spinach
- 1/2 cup tomatoes, diced
- 4 cups whole grain pasta, cooked
- 1/4 cup shredded parmesan

How to prepare:

In skillet, heat oil to medium heat. Add shrimp, garlic, onion, zucchini, and eggplant. Cook until shrimp just begins to firm and veggies are soft. Add capers, spinach, and tomato. Cook until spinach is wilted and tomatoes are hot. Toss in pasta, continue to simmer until pasta is heated through. Top with shredded parmesan

Total calories: 517

Vitamins: Vitamin A 184 µg, Vitamin B6 0.5mg, Vitamin B12 1.6µg, Vitamin K 88µg

Minerals: Calcium 360mg, Magnesium 132mg, Phosphorus 598mg, Selenium 97µg, Zink 4mg

Sugars: 5g

37. Paprika Chicken with Beans and Quinoa

This well rounded chicken entrée is a great source of iron. Iron is directly connects to brain health and functions. Not only does iron assist in proper blood flow, it creates neural pathways to help with the prevention of cognitive decline.

Ingredients:

- 1 tablespoon olive oil
- 2 boneless skinless chicken breast, cut into cubes
- 2 tablespoons Paprika
- 2 clove garlic, minced
- 2 cups fresh green beans, trimmed
- 1 cup butter beans
- 1/2 cup cashews
- 2 cups quinoa, cooked

How to prepare:

Add olive oil to skillet and heat on medium. Add chicken and cook until no pink remains. Mix in paprika, garlic and green beans. Continue to cook until beans just begin to soften. Stir in butter beans and cashews. Serve alongside cooked quinoa.

Total calories: 714

Vitamins: Vitamin A 199µg, Vitamin B6 1.1mg, Vitamin B12 1µg, Vitamin K 63µg

Minerals: Iron 8mg, Magnesium 247mg, Phosphorus 803mg, and Selenium 77mg, Zinc 6mg

Sugars: 7g

38. Spinach and Pesto Fettuccini with Sundried Tomatoes

A little used ingredient, sundried tomatoes contain higher amounts of Vitamin C and A than raw tomatoes. Both vitamins C and A protect brain cells from free radical damage and are and excellent way to improve overall brain health.

Ingredients:

- 1 tablespoon olive oil
- 2 clove garlic, minced
- 1 cup sundried tomatoes
- 2 cups spinach
- 1/2 pound whole wheat fettuccini, cooked
- 2 tablespoons basil pesto
- 1/4 cup shredded parmesan

How to prepare:

Heat olive oil over medium temperature. Add garlic and sundried tomatoes. Cook until fragrant, add spinach and continue cooking until wilted. Add fettuccini and pesto.

Toss to coat in pesto, heat until hot. Divide onto serving dishes, top with parmesan.

Total calories: 464

Vitamins: Vitamin A 187μg, Vitamin C 21mg, Vitamin K 178 μg

Minerals: Magnesium 139mg, Phosphorus 365mg, Selenium 47μg, Zinc 3mg

Sugars: 12g

39. Seared Halibut with Red Cabbage

Combining Halibut and Cabbage in this crisp fresh entrée create a super force of brain boosting vitamins and minerals. Red cabbage is a powerful antiaging source while Halibut is packed with OMEGA3s and B Vitamins to give the brain extra energy.

Ingredients:

- 2 tablespoon olive oil, divided
- 1 teaspoon ground turmeric
- 1/2 teaspoon ground cumin
- 1/2 teaspoon salt
- 1/2 teaspoon cayenne pepper
- 2 (6oz) Halibut filets
- 1 bulb fennel, sliced
- 1 small red onion, sliced thin
- 2 cups red cabbage, shredded
- 3 tablespoons pine nuts
- 1 large orange, peeled and cut into wedges

How to prepare:

Heat half olive oil on medium in skillet. Mix together turmeric, cumin, salt, and cayenne. Season Halibut with spice mix and lay in hot olive oil. Once brown, flip and cook second side until flaky and cooked through. Remove fish from pan and set aside.

In the same pan, add the remaining olive oil, if necessary. Add fennel, onion and cabbage. Lightly cook until the vegetables just begin to lose their crunch. Add pine nuts and orange. Place on serving dish and top with Halibut.

Total calories: 491

Vitamins: Vitamin A 144µg, Vitamin B6 0.6mg, Vitamin B12 3.1µg, Vitamin C 68mg, Vitamin D 8µg, Vitamin E 6mg, Vitamin K 123µg

Minerals: Magnesium 127mg, Phosphorus 900mg, Selenium 78µg, Choline 228mg

Sugars: 10g

40. Chicken, Olives, and Tomato with Spinach Herb Orzo

Combining olives, tomatoes, and spinach in this entrée create a powerhouse of anti-inflammatory agents. Increasing blood flow and providing brain cells with the oxygen they need, each of these ingredients should be consumed on a regular basis.

Ingredients:

- 1 tablespoon olive oil
- 1 tablespoon lemon juice
- 1 tablespoon dried oregano
- 1 clove garlic, minced
- 2 boneless skinless chicken breast
- 1 tomato, diced
- 1/4 cup black olives
- 2 cups orzo, cooked
- 1/2 cup spinach
- 1 teaspoon fresh basil, chopped
- 1 teaspoon fresh rosemary, chopped

How to prepare:

Combine oil, lemon juice, oregano and garlic. Pour over chicken. Chill for 30 minutes

In skillet on medium heat, place chicken. Cook the first side just until brown, flip. While cooking second side add tomatoes and olives. Gently stir without flipping chicken. Once chicken is cook through, remove from heat.

In second pan, add orzo, spinach, basil, and rosemary. Cook until spinach is wilted and orzo heated through. Spoon on to serving plate. Top with chicken, tomato, and olives.

Total calories: 675

Vitamins: Vitamin B6 1.4mg, Vitamin K 70μg

Minerals: Phosphorus 569mg, Selenium 97mg, Zinc 3mg, Thiamin 0.6mg, Riboflavin 0.5mg, Niacin 30mg, Choline 189mg

Sugars: 3g

41. Warm Kale Salad with Lemon Vinaigrette

Pairing kale with lemon creates a powerful food combination. Not only does the lemon balance the bold flavor of kale, it combines iron with Vitamin C. This improves absorption of both iron and Vitamin C allowing the body to obtain full benefits of both supplements.

Ingredients:

- 1 tablespoon olive oil
- 1/2 cup zucchini, diced
- 1/2 cup eggplant, diced
- 1/2 cup tomato, diced
- 3 cup kale, chopped
- 1 cup spinach, chopped
- 1/2 cup walnuts, chopped
- 1 tablespoon honey
- 2 tablespoons lemon juice

How to prepare:

In skillet, heat olive oil. On medium heat, add zucchini, eggplant, and tomato. Cook until soft.

Toss kale and spinach together and divide between serving bowls. Top with zucchini mix and walnuts

In small bowl, whisk together honey and lemon juice. Drizzle over salad and serve.

Total calories: 521

Vitamins: Vitamin A 340µg, Vitamin B6 1mg, Vitamin C 78mg, Vitamin K 431µg

Minerals: Magnesium 116mg, Phosphorus 404mg, Selenium 50µg

Sugars: 8g

ADDITIONAL TITLES FROM THIS AUTHOR

70 Effective Meal Recipes to Prevent and Solve Being Overweight: Burn Fat Fast by Using Proper Dieting and Smart Nutrition

By

Joe Correa CSN

48 Acne Solving Meal Recipes: The Fast and Natural Path to Fixing Your Acne Problems in Less Than 10 Days!

By

Joe Correa CSN

41 Alzheimer's Preventing Meal Recipes: Reduce or Eliminate Your Alzheimer's Condition in 30 Days or Less!

By

Joe Correa CSN

70 Effective Breast Cancer Meal Recipes: Prevent and Fight Breast Cancer with Smart Nutrition and Powerful Foods

By

Joe Correa CSN

www.ingramcontent.com/pod-product-compliance
Lightning Source LLC
Chambersburg PA
CBHW070153080526
44586CB00015B/1970